TRINIDAD&TOBAGO

TRINIDAD&TOBAGO

CARNIVAL LAND WATER PEOPLE

Macmillan Education

Between Towns Road, Oxford OX4 3PP

A division of Macmillan Publishers Limited

Companies and representatives throughout the world

www.macmillan-caribbean.com

ISBN-13: 978-1-4050-0749-8

ISBN-10: 1-4050-0749-4

Text © Jeremy Taylor 2006

Photographs © Alex Smailes 2006

Maps © Macmillan Publishers Limited 2006

First published 2006

Designed by Gareth Jenkins / ABOVE, Trinidad & Tobago

Maps by Peter Harper / Gareth Jenkins

The authors and publishers would like to thank the following for permission to reproduce their photographs:

Abigail Hadeed: back flap

Stephen Broadbridge: pp. 45,46,47,48,48,49,50,89,102

EMPICS: pp. 158,159

Shirley Bahadur/Trinidad Guardian: p. 160

All other photographs were supplied by the authors.

The author and publishers would like to thank the following for permission to reproduce their material:

Earl Lovelace for the extract from *The Dragon Can't Dance* by Earl Lovelace; Merle Hodge for the extract from "The Peoples of Trinidad & Tobago" by Merle Hodge in *David Frost introduces Trinidad & Tobago* ed. by Anthony and Carr; Picador for the extract from *Tide Running* by Oonya Kempadoo.

The publishers have made every effort to trace the copyright holders, but if they have inadvertently overlooked any, they will be pleased to make the necessary arrangements at the first opportunity.

Printed and bound in Thailand

2009 2008 2007 2006

10 9 8 7 6 5 4 3 2 1

CONTENTS

TRINIDAD

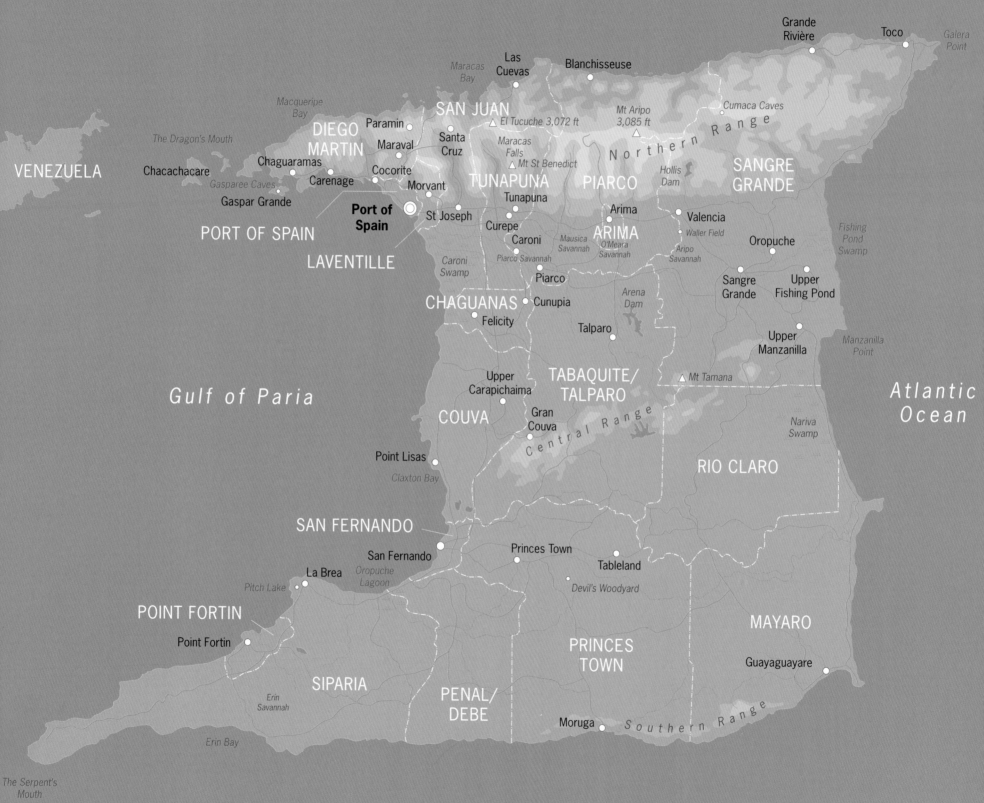

Caribbean Sea

Grande Rivière
Toco
Galera Point

Maracas Bay
Las Cuevas
Blanchisseuse

Macqueripe Bay
The Dragon's Mouth
SAN JUAN
Mt Aripo 3,085 ft
Cumaca Caves
Northern Range

DIEGO MARTIN
Paramin
Santa Cruz
El Tucuche 3,072 ft
Maracas Falls
Mt St Benedict
Hollis Dam
SANGRE GRANDE

VENEZUELA
Chacachacare
Chaguaramas
Maraval
Cocorite
Carenage
Morvant
TUNAPUNA
PIARCO
Gaspar Grande
Gasparee Caves
Tunapuna
Arima
Valencia
Fishing Pond Swamp

PORT OF SPAIN
Port of Spain
St Joseph
Curepe
Caroni
ARIMA
Waller Field
Oropuche

LAVENTILLE
Caroni Swamp
Piarco Savannah
Mausica Savannah
O'Meara Savannah
Aripo Savannah
Sangre Grande
Upper Fishing Pond

CHAGUANAS
Cunupia
Piarco
Arena Dam
Upper Manzanilla
Manzanilla Point

Felicity
Talparo

Gulf of Paria
Upper Carapichaima
TABAQUITE/ TALPARO
Mt Tamana
Nariva Swamp

COUVA
Gran Couva
Central Range

Atlantic Ocean

Point Lisas
Claxton Bay
RIO CLARO

SAN FERNANDO
San Fernando
Princes Town
Tableland

La Brea
Oropuche Lagoon
Devil's Woodyard

POINT FORTIN
Pitch Lake

Point Fortin
MAYARO
Guayaguayare

SIPARIA
Erin Savannah
PENAL/ DEBE
PRINCES TOWN
Moruga
Southern Range

Erin Bay

The Serpent's Mouth

Columbus Channel

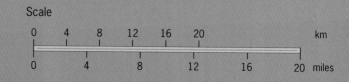

Scale

| 0 | 4 | 8 | 12 | 16 | 20 | km |

| 0 | 4 | 8 | 12 | 16 | 20 miles |

x

TOBAGO

St Giles Island

Caribbean Sea

Man O'War
Bay

Charlotteville

Englishman's
Bay

Tobago
Forest
Reserve

Pigeon Peak
△

Speyside

Little Tobago

M a i n   R i d g e

Culloden
Bay

Argyle Falls

Argyle

Roxborough

Moriah

Hillsborough
Dam

Glamorgan

Plymouth

Buccoo
Reef

Nylon Pool

Buccoo

Bon
Accord
Lagoon

Buccoo
Bay

Pigeon
Point

Hillsborough
Bay

Store Bay

Mount
Pleasant

Scarborough

Bon Accord

Little Rockly
Bay

Crown
Point

Canoe
Bay

Atlantic Ocean

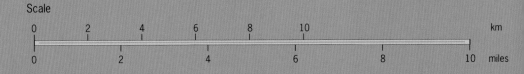

Scale

| 0 | | 2 | | 4 | | 6 | | 8 | | 10 | | km |

| 0 | | 2 | | 4 | | 6 | | 8 | | 10 miles |

But the real losers were the first settlers, the Aruacs and Caribs. A small community of Caribs does survive, in Arima and across the mountains in coastal Paria, though there has been a good deal of mixed blood over the generations. They are virtually forgotten by the rest of the community, even though elemental Caribbean words (hammock, barbecue, hurricane) come from them, and graceful Amerindian place names still survive (Tunapuna, Mucurapo, Carapichaima, Guayaguayare). Still presided over by a queen and maintaining links with other surviving communities (in Dominica, St Vincent and Venezuela, for example), the Caribs do have their own festival – the Santa Rosa Festival in August – but it really commemorates their conversion to Catholicism rather than their survival as an independent, organic people and culture.

It was the Catholic French who brought Carnival to Trinidad in the 1780s, when the island was trying to attract a population. For them, it was an elegant and decorous affair, planters and their families donning masks and costumes and riding about in carriages. The French mimicked their servants and slaves, and the compliment was secretly returned with interest – the figure of the Dame Lorraine with her stupendous bust can still be seen today.

But after emancipation in the 1830s the tables were turned, and the Africans took Carnival onto the streets. For the rest of the century the festivities grew noisier, rowdier and more riotous, not merely to let off steam but specifically to demoralise the French and English establishment. The English were never great Carnival lovers anyway, and were easily upset by mass disorder and impropriety. The forerunners of today's mas' (masquerade) bands surged through the streets, the *chantuelle* (forerunner of today's calypsonian) leading the music and broadcasting news, gossip, satire and scandal that caused city matrons to block their ears more tightly than ever.

In 1884 the British ran out of patience and banned African drumming, the main source of music for the bands. But after some experimentation a substitute was found: long sticks of bamboo cut to varying lengths and thumped on the ground in a drumlike rhythm. It produced a highly rhythmic, almost sinister sound. The differing lengths, musicians noted, could deliver different sounds and pitches.

As time went on, the songs of the *chantuelles* – now delivered in English rather than French patois – seemed too good to miss, and the first calypso 'tents' were established, where folks could sit down and listen to a series of performances and enjoy all of them, rather than just their own band's. A long battle with the colonial censor (who couldn't understand much of what was being sung anyway) loomed.

Soon, other makeshift material was being added to the joyous Carnival cacophony: the hubs of car wheels, biscuit tins, oil drums (Trinidad's oil industry, one of the oldest in the world, had started up in 1857). It was not long before musicians realised that the oil drums – rather like the bamboo – could be cut, and their ends beaten and moulded to produce specific notes. And so the steel pan was born, the African drum rebirthed out of western industrial waste, and musicians in east Port of Spain tapped out rudimentary

melodies. At first the 'pans' were slung around the neck and played rather like side drums in a military band, but later a full orchestral range of pans – from deep-voiced cellos to melody-carrying tenors – was mounted on wheeled racks that could be pushed through the streets or onto the competition stage.

It took a good while for this new instrument to gain acceptance from middle-class colonial Trinidad, but its appearance in London at the 1951 Festival of Britain signalled victory, and today it is unthinkable for even the most diehard reactionary to express distaste for pan. It is the official 'national instrument', and is often claimed to be the only new musical instrument invented in the twentieth century (this is not true, but the pan has a fair claim to be the century's only acoustic, i.e. non-electronic, invention).

The wild colonial Carnival was eventually tamed by competition and money. Today's steel orchestras still have to figure out how to be profitable businesses; they depend on commercial sponsors and government-funded prizes and appearance fees for survival. The masquerade bands obediently follow prescribed routes through the city, passing obligatory judging points in their quest for titles and prizes. Calypsonians from the tents jostle to reach the finals of the Calypso Monarch competition where they can win desirable rewards like a new car.

But the old dichotomy, half-consciously, survives. Today's 'pretty mas' – hordes of beautiful women in bikini-based costumes, with smaller numbers of muscled men in attendance – has to do with physical and sexual display as well as emotional release. But 'J'Ouvert' – the ritual that actually begins the Carnival early on Monday morning – takes place in the dark before dawn, and has to do with the grotesque and the bizarre, satire and surprise, fear and defiance. No pretty costumes here: J'Ouvert people are smeared all over with mud, paint, oil or grease. They peddle awful puns, they are cross-dressers, they brandish diabolical pitchforks. J'Ouvert revellers turn the normal upside down and inside out; they evoke the old canboulay (cannes brulées) sorties when slaves had to turn out to deal with burning sugar fields. Light and dark: it's as if France and Africa are still fighting the battles of 200 years ago.

The traditional 'characters' of Carnival have almost disappeared except in special 'old-times' performances: the prancing devils and imps, the broad-winged bats and the Midnight Robbers with their incomprehensible speeches, the Moko Jumbies on their stilts, the doleful Minstrels, the solemn Bookmen, the Wild Indians, the jab-jabs (diables) and the pierrots. But the bigger bands still have their kings and queens, huge extravaganzas seeking to impress through colour and design, complexity, 'research', and (more recently) special effects such as dramatic lighting, smoke and pyrotechnics.

The Carnival season fêtes have changed a lot too: once fairly easy-going social affairs, they are now mostly all-night marathons for the hyperactive young who are roused to frenzy by the decibels from the speakers and the athletic sexuality and dynamism of the latter-day chantuelles as they shriek instructions from the stage.

Carnival sucks up so much of the country's creative energy that the other arts tend to suffer by comparison. But there is a lot of good work going on among visual artists, in theatre, and in fashion design; and Trinidad and Tobago has a long literary tradition that produced (among others) V. S. Naipaul (Nobel Prize for Literature), Earl Lovelace (Commonwealth Writers Prize) and Sam Selvon. Trinidad architects have created some very tasteful restorations and striking new buildings in Port of Spain, sometimes trying to synthesize post-modern design with indigenous tradition. Film has yet to find a foothold, though there are several young film-makers whose problem is capital rather than skill; indigenous television, after a long drought when screens were completely dominated by US cable, is only now trying to make some sort of comeback.

But Carnival is not the only glue holding creole culture together. People don African outfits for Emancipation Day in August, commemorating the end of enslavement, and Indian outfits for Arrival Day in March, marking the landing of the first Indian workers. Divali, the Hindu festival of lights in October/November, strikes a chord in all communities, its flickering deyas (oil lamps) decorating homes as well as public roads and buildings and parks. The Muslim Hosay also attracts a cross-section of people now: although it is strictly a ritual of mourning for the grandson of the Prophet and his brother, killed at the Battle of Kerbala in 680 (and stricter Muslims frown on its departure from that), Hosay is now an impressive four-night procession with thunderous tassa drumming, dancers twirling twelve-foot moons on their shoulders; flags still represent the battle, and huge tadzehs, decorated floats representing the martyrs' tombs, are carried through the streets. People of all communities join in, giving the processions a Carnival flavour.

There is a similar crossover in the Indian spring festival of Phagwah, where even politicians feel it necessary to join the crowd and get drenched in purple abeer (coloured powder). For Eid-ul-Fitr, which ends the fasting month of Ramadan, Muslims invite friends of any background to join the table.

Cross-cultural interaction is probably most obvious at the moment in music, the art at which Trinidad and Tobago most excels. Traditional calypso, with its easy-going beat and playful lyrics, has been speeding up now for three decades, turning into fast, high-energy dance music in which lyrics have little importance – nobody really needs the calypsonian any more for comment, analysis or comedy (there are newspapers, the TV and comedy shows for that), so the music ('soca') is for dancing; and you have to be pretty fit to keep up with its frenetic beat.

Into soca has crept a powerful Indian flavour from traditional and rather naughty Hindu 'chutney' music, so you not only have calypso but soca and chutney soca as well. From Jamaica comes the influence of reggae and dancehall, from Orisha ('Shango') and the Baptists the feel of deep-rooted African chant, and from the United States the flavour of rap, incorporated some time ago into Trinidadian music to form a distinctive local 'rapso'. In the music of a singer-composer like David Rudder, or a group like 3-Canal, you can hear all these influences at work.

Towards Christmas everything gives way to *parang*, the Latin-flavoured carols from Venezuela which are sung still in Spanish. But parang has already flirted with soca and given birth to parang-soca. And so it goes on: Spain, France, England, Africa, India, China, the Levant (yes, there are Chinese and Syrian calypsonians), Jamaica, Brooklyn, all drawn into that joyously hybrid thing that is Trinidadian creole music.

A similar process has taken place in the nation's kitchens. Creole cooking embraces good ideas from almost anywhere and adapts them to local tastes: Africa, the Caribbean plantation, India, China and the Middle East have all left their mark. You can't not have some pelau, people will tell you, or some rice-and-peas, some souse, ham-and-hops, callaloo, buljol, sancoche or cow-heel soup. You can't go to Maracas Beach without eating a shark-and-bake, or to Tobago without finishing a hefty plate of curry-crab-and-dumpling. Cold coconuts and corn soup around the Savannah are among life's essentials. Roti (curry folded in a dough wrapping, probably the world's tastiest snack) and doubles (curried channa in a soft dough case) are hugely popular Indian contributions, as are Christmas pastelles and arepas from the Spanish, wantons from the Chinese, kibbis and hummus from the Syrians and Lebanese, and fast foods of every conceivable origin.

Trinidad makes remarkably good rums and beers; sorrel and ginger beer and ponche-à-crème are indispensable at Christmas, and nobody would dream of not having Angostura bitters in the kitchen, since it is made up the road in Laventille (the Prussian inventor, Dr Johann Siegert, having developed it as a stomach-settler for Simon Bolivar's army during the Venezuelan revolutionary war, and later retreated to Trinidad to manufacture it).

The other main area of creole commonality, sport, involves pretty much everyone. Cricket is still big, and – since neither France nor Spain play the game – victory over England, the colonial 'mother country' and inventor of the game, is a sweet triumph when it comes. The legendary Brian Lara, who broke all the top batting records in the game, is Trinidadian. The national football squad (the Soca Warriors) is eternally optimistic about getting into the World Cup finals, and young athletes hammer on the doors of the Olympic Games – another Trinidadian, Hasely Crawford, won the 100 metres gold in 1976, and his compatriot Ato Boldon has come close to doing the same. Some sports – basketball, rugby, sailing, tennis, golf, volleyball, game fishing, surfing – you would expect in a Caribbean island nation; others you might not – horse racing, drag racing, power boat racing, kick-boxing, taekwondo, martial arts.

Tobago's cultural heritage is fundamentally different from Trinidad's; its showcase is the Tobago Heritage Festival, held in July–August. Audiences travel from village to village: each community is responsible for a different aspect of the tradition – storytelling here, food there, dances somewhere else. A traditional Tobago wedding is re-enacted in Moriah, with the groom decked out in old-fashioned top-hat and scissor-tailed coat; the wedding procession proceeds to the music of fiddle and tambourine (Tobago has been more generous in retaining and adapting English dances and rhythms than Trinidad has).

Tobago has a unique Eastertime ritual, said to have been the island's answer to Port of Spain's puffed-up horse-racing crowd many decades ago. It races goats and crabs instead. The goats can fairly easily be guided in the right direction over a hundred-yard course by their 'jockeys', even though they can't actually be ridden and, like all goats, can show surprisingly stubborn and perverse instincts. The crabs are hopelessly wayward, however, preferring sideways to forward movement, and it can take quite a while to complete a ten-foot race. Bets are taken, just as with the horses, and a good deal of drinking is understandably done.

Tobago has made its own accommodation with the creolisation process, keeping its distance from Trinidad in some things, and often adapting Trinidadian creolism to its own needs (like the Carnival-style Tobago Fest, held in September). But both islands are part of a mainstream culture now, strengthening identity and selfhood through it. Often people do not realise just how much they do share: Trinidadians and Tobagonians who at home might be aware only of their differences, when they meet overseas remember only what they have in common, the unspoken things they are instinctively nostalgic for.

Coming to terms with the land itself is another part of the slow process of decolonisation. For so long the land belonged to someone else and people were forced to work it. Afterwards they mistrusted or resented the land, felt they were camping on it, or merely passing through (as many families have actually done, moving on from the Caribbean to the greener pastures of North America or the 'mother country').

But the land itself was there long before people or trampling colonisers. Because it was once part of the vast continent to the south, it is rich in life forms like the mainland; yet because it is now islands, it has acquired island forms too. In a small, easily accessible area, it takes the form of tropical forests and reefs, mountains and plains, mangrove and swamp, rainforest and rivers, seashore and tropical savannah, all close to each other.

The atlas shows just how obviously Trinidad is part of South America, sliced off by narrow flooded channels. Its savannah lands are an extension of the *llanos* of central Venezuela; its Northern Range is part of the great South American *cordillera*. Look at the line of the continental shelf, the 200-fathom line, and see how it just curls around the northern tip of Tobago before cutting away sharply to the south.

These are tropical islands, with an average mean daily maximum of 32˚C, and two main seasons caused by the northward and southward drift of the Intertropical Convergence Zone, which brings rainfall from June to the end of the year and usually allows the land to dry up in the early months.

About a quarter of the country is still forested, far less than when the stubborn Genoese appeared. The flora is both native and introduced, with 2,500 species in 175 families. There are 300 different ferns, 700 orchids. Vivid purple and yellow poui trees and

spectacular red immortelles splash colour along the hillsides. The most casual observer can begin to recognise the different species of palm, the almond, banyan and breadfruit, flamboyant and cassia, African tulip, silk cotton, matchwood and teak, mora and poui. Gardens blaze with amaryllis lilies and yellow allamanda, hibiscus and Turk's cap, chaconia and bougainvillea, giant anthuriums, and heliconias, like the lobster claw.

The fauna includes over 430 bird species counting migrants (this is a major crossroads on the migration paths of birds moving both north and south); more than 250 breed in the islands. Two hundred of the species are recorded in Tobago. The 600 listed butterflies increase to over 1,000 if moths and skipper butterflies are included; about 670 vertebrates are recorded, in 137 families, and 100 mammals. Only 4 of the 47 snakes are venomous (and none of those inhabit Tobago).

The forest is home to a surprising number of wild animals, including the agouti, paca (known locally as the lappe), armadillo (tatoo), opossum (manicou), deer, peccary or wild pig (quenk), tayra (wild dog or *chien bois*), ocelot (tiger cat) and anteater. Amazon parrots, iguanas, manatees, capuchin and howler monkeys are easily sighted. Frogs and toads abound, never bothering to mute their raucous calls during the wet season.

Among the most memorable sights are the huge leatherback turtles which heave themselves out of the water to nest on their ancestral beaches, digging holes in the sand and crouching trance-like while their eggs are freed, before crawling back into the dark waters. Their phenomenal navigation and their prehistoric form make them some of the most intriguing creatures to be found anywhere. In the Caroni Swamp on Trinidad's west coast, flocks of brilliant scarlet ibis fly home in the evening to roost. At La Brea, a deep well of churning bitumen oozing from a subterranean fault forms an endlessly self-renewing Pitch Lake, its contents used for road and roof surfacing in many countries. You can walk on the surface, carefully, not standing too long in any one spot.

In several areas of South Trinidad are small mud volcanoes, like the Devil's Woodyard, a short way south of Princes Town. In the limestone caves of the Northern Range, oilbirds wheel through the dark caverns uttering the sharp, high-pitched clicks of their navigation system. The bat caves of Mount Tamana, sightless fish, fishing bats, a unique golden tree frog found high on El Tucuche, the almost extinct bush turkey or pawi – these are some of the results of Trinidad and Tobago's on-and-off flirtation with South America.

The relationship continues today; though in relatively subdued manner. The waters of the great Orinoco flood into the Atlantic not far to the south of Trinidad, feeding the north-moving Guyana Current which divides around Trinidad, but washes the south and east coasts of Tobago. This provides nutrients to support a diversity of marine life unusual even for the prolific Caribbean. Deep-sea fish are found here much closer to the surface than normal; barracudas, dolphins, whale sharks, turtles, porpoises and manta rays are common. Smaller fish abound – butterfly fish, queen and French angels, damsels, parrotfish, grunts. Rare species such as tarpon and trigger fish are regular residents.

One major reef – Buccoo – is easily accessible even to non-swimmers, while for scuba-divers there are outstanding reef formations along the west and north-east coasts. All the known hard corals and most of the soft ones can be found around Tobago, including the world's largest known brain coral, 12 feet high and 16 feet across. Four species of nesting turtles – the green, loggerhead and hawksbill, as well as the endangered leatherback – nest on local beaches.

Pipelines, oil rigs and industrial plant don't make exciting subjects for a photographer. But there are other signs of unexpected affluence in these islands: traffic jams, the number of new cars on the road, the extravagance of some of the richer suburbs, the colonies of expatriate managers with foreign accents.

From our vantage point on Lady Young Road, above Port of Spain, the liquefied natural gas tankers moving endlessly in and out of the gas liquefaction terminals at Point Fortin are probably invisible in the heat haze (they supply most of the United States's imported LNG). So are the monster gas-fuelled plants at Point Lisas near San Fernando – steel, ammonia, methanol, urea – which have taken root where once sugar was grown as a colonial export commodity. Further still down the coast, a new industrial estate is taking shape at La Brea. The oil below the rolling southern hills is hidden, of course, as are the gas and oil fields beneath the seabed off every coastline – but not the oil rigs relentlessly searching for them and pumping their contents back to shore.

It is this energy wealth that has given Trinidad and Tobago the strongest economy in the Caribbean. Trinidad's greatest piece of good fortune since the shattering of its pre-Columbian world in 1498 has been to share this part of the planet with its neighbour Venezuela, straddling one of the biggest energy reservoirs on the planet. Trinidad has been making money from oil since the 1860s, and since 1980 has been monetising its reserves by using natural gas to generate electricity and run a formidable cluster of petrochemical industries. None of its neighbours in the Caribbean has anything like the same potential strengths and opportunities, only the fickle rewards of tourism and agriculture to fall back on.

Money, of course, is no cure-all. Trinidad and Tobago's problems – growing crime, HIV/AIDS, drugs, poverty, the globalisation shock, restructuring needs – are not solved: whose are? But the ambitious national goal is to pursue such far-reaching social change that by 2020 Trinidad and Tobago will be able to call itself a developed nation. The fate of that idea will show whether the country's oil and gas wealth turns out to be a blessing or a curse.

Jeremy Taylor

Jeremy Taylor
Port of Spain, 2005

CARNIVAL

The Dragon
Can't Dance,
Earl Lovelace (1979)

In truth, it was in the spirit of priesthood that Aldrick addressed his work; for the making of his dragon costume was to him always a new miracle, a new test not only of his skill but his faith: for though he knew exactly what he had to do, it was only by faith that he could bring alive from these scraps of cloth and tin that dragon, its mouth breathing fire, its tail threshing the ground, its nine chains rattling, that would contain the beauty and threat and terror that was the message he took each year to Port of Spain. It was in this message that he asserted before the world his self. It was through it that he demanded that others see him, recognize his personhood, be warned of his dangerousness.

Not as quiet as
you might think:
creatures you might
meet in the village
of Paramin, in the
hills north of Port of
Spain, on a Carnival
Monday night.

Around the Queen's Park Savannah,
food vendors serve local dishes
and cold drinks to weary revellers.

Previous Pent-up energy is released with the
crossing of the Queen's Park Savannah stage,
Carnival Central for masqueraders, spectators
and TV viewers.

Above Big Carnival bands provide communal catharsis through thunderous music, instinctive movement and vivid colour.

Overleaf Poison in full flood. The largest bands now attract well over 10,000 masqueraders, provide mobile restrooms, and may split into several different entities.

Partygoers at a 'Bacchanal Wednesday' fête staged by Club Coconuts in Chaguaramas.

ack-up dancers
ke this celebrated
erformer for
lachel Montano
re essential to the
arnival action.

Soca favourites.
Clockwise from top left **Gypsy delivers classic calypso ... Soca Elvis wines low ...**
while Rikki Jai blends quality calypso with contemporary and Indian rhythms.

An unbeatable duet: the
Mighty Sparrow and Calypso
Rose battle it out on stage.

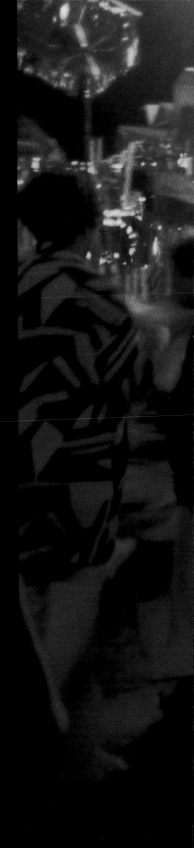

Panorama is the fiercest test for steel orchestras. Players – young and old, men and women – have been rehearsing nightly in the panyards for weeks before the final night.

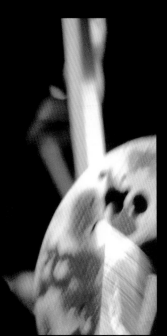

LAND

*At Last: A Christmas
in the West Indies,*
Charles Kingsley (1871)

I have seen them at last. I have been at last in the High Woods, as the primeval forest is known here; and they are not less, but more, wonderful than I had imagined them . . . My first feeling on entering the high woods was helplessness, confusion, awe, all but terror. One is afraid at first to venture in fifty yards . . . You can only wander on as far as you dare, letting each object impress itself upon your mind as it may, and carrying away a confused recollection of innumerable perpendicular lines, all straining upwards, in fierce competition, towards the light-food far above . . .

At 3,072 feet, El Tucuche, in the Northern Range, is the second highest point in Trinidad. El Cerro del Aripo, a few miles to the east, is just 13 feet higher.

Forest canopy on the lower mountain slopes.

Stephen Broadbridge

The crested oropendola makes these strange suspended homes, which can be seen all over both islands.

Stephen Broadbrie

Male and female purple honeycreepers are
common forest residents in Trinidad, and also
like cocoa and citrus plantations.

Stephen Broadbridge

Hummingbirds are among the most fascinating residents of both islands. Swift, agile, fiercely independent, they can hover and even fly backwards; their wings can beat up to 70 or 80 times a second.

Stephen Broadbridge

The blue-and-gold
macaw has been
fighting against
extinction.

The impressive white
hawk usually hunts
from a perch or while
gliding from a low level.

Stephen Broadbridge

Red howler monkeys are noisy
residents of Trinidad's forests.

White-faced capuchins
are notoriously curious.

Sheeba, a university graduate and the only local scientist to
specialise in rainforest canopies, is seen here in her natural habitat.

From left In mountainous rainforests, mosses and ferns thrive on the constant rainfall and cooler temperatures ... Lianas climb a forest tree to reach daylight; they may one day strangle and kill their host ... A young fern slowly emerges ... Layers of plants scramble for precious space in the rainforest.

Top left Camouflage is one of nature's most ingenious ideas. Here a hummingbird moth, so called for its narrow wings and high wing beat, finds bark to blend with.

Below left This harlequin beetle has a camouflaged back and long legs looking like twigs.

Top right A moth finds similarly coloured leaves to hide against.

Below right *Anolis chrysolepis*'s camouflage is so good he believes himself to be invisible, and will stay still in this position for a long time.

A moth imitates
a leaf.

A leaf-cutting ant transports fungus.

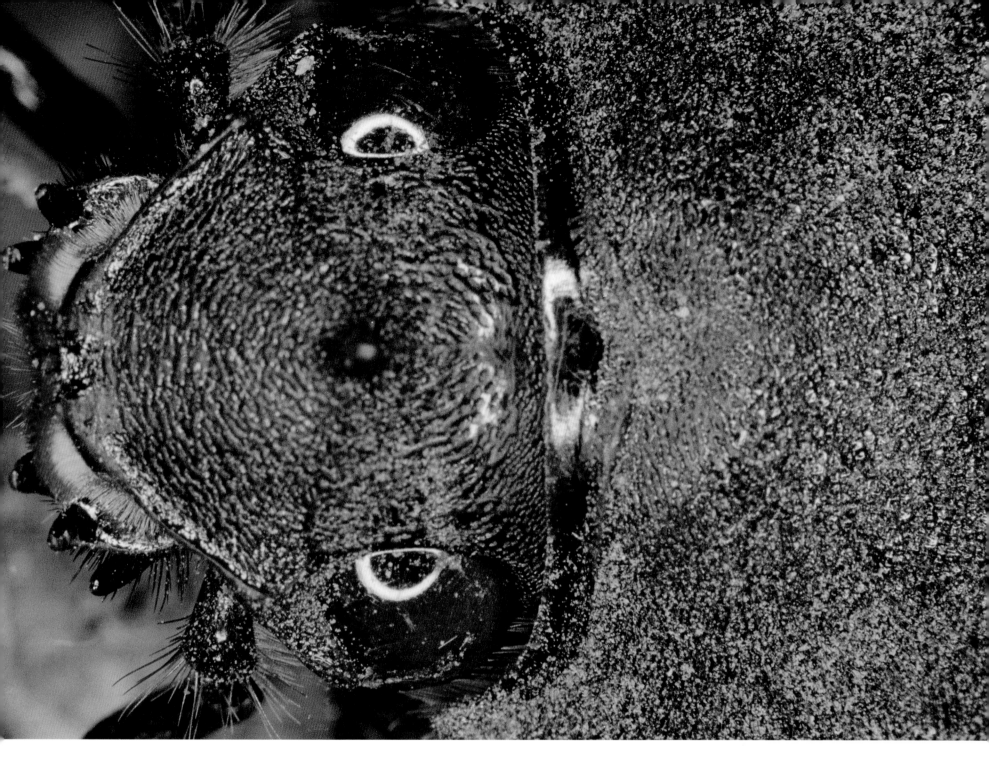

A female rhino beetle.

Below Seed pods, carried by animals
and birds, are the germination system for
many trees and plants.

Right Falling leaves
make way for new
growth.

Overleaf
Everyday beauty.

Boa constrictor.

The harmless yellow-
belly puffer snake.

Cook's tree boa.

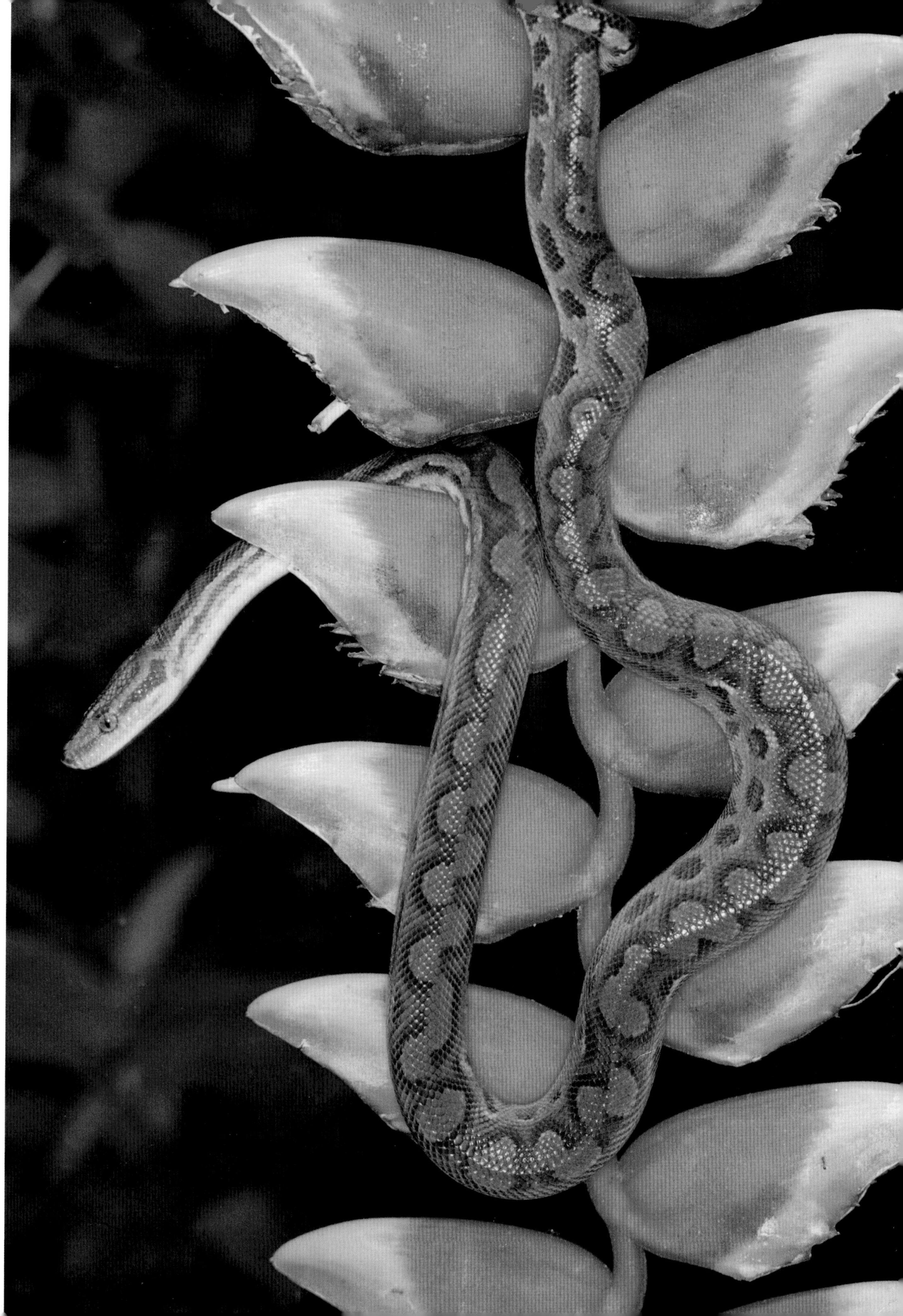

Right A rainbow boa on an ornamental heliconia.

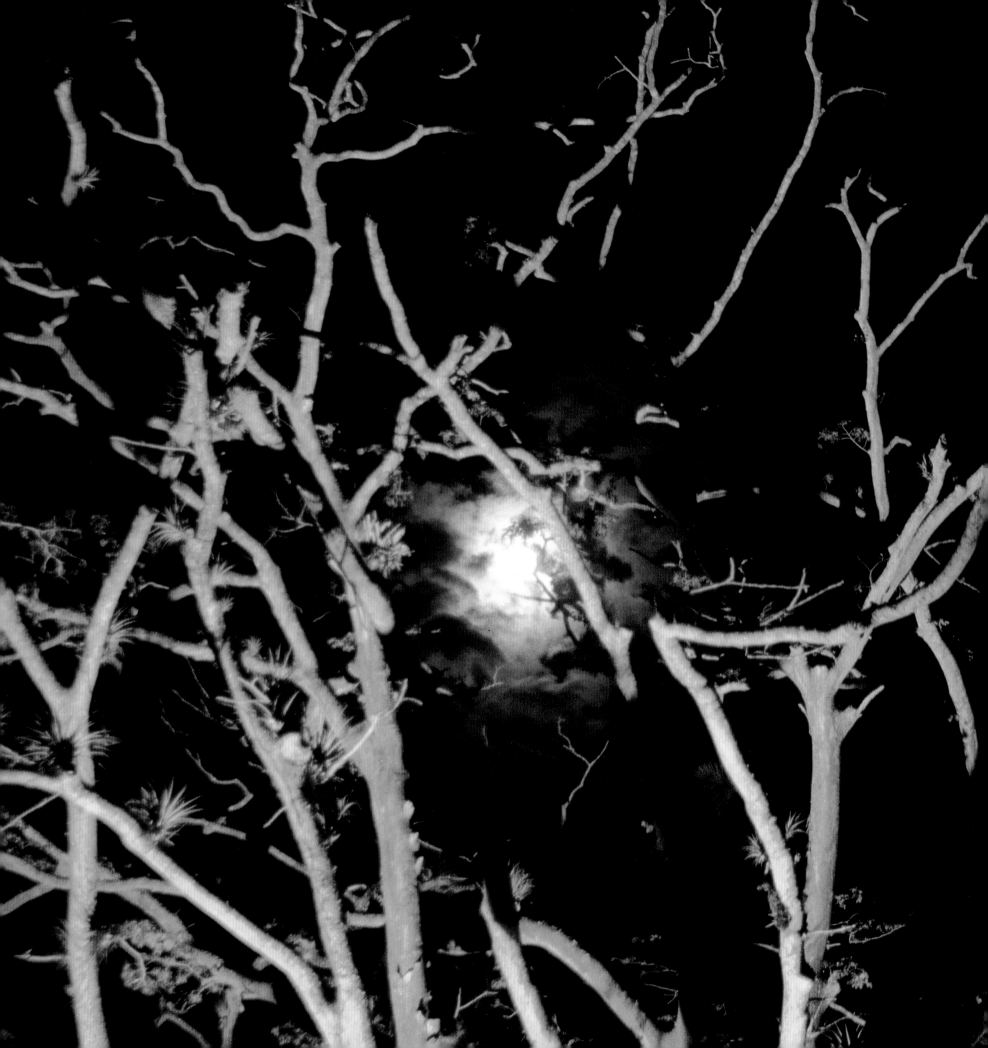

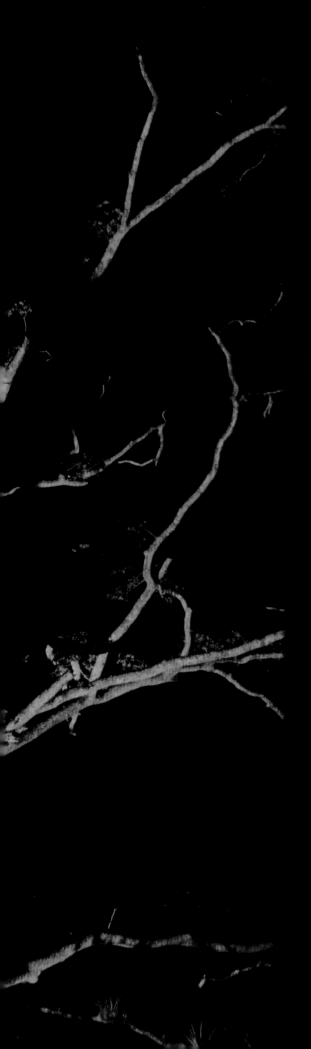

Left **Beyond this samaan tree, in the moonlight, a whole new world of wildlife stirs.**

Things that sting... Right **Centipedes are found under dry wood and leaves.**

The bird-eating spider sometimes makes itself comfortable in country homes, but is harmless unless interfered with.

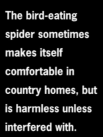

Scorpions like old logs and fallen trees.

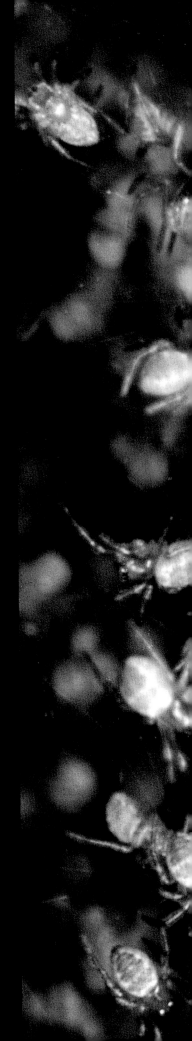

Right **During mating, the male spider performs a special dance so the female recognises him as the same species and does not consume him.**

Left **Multiple strands of silk immobilise prey quickly. During normal web building, thinner concentrations are used.**

Venom is injected into the prey, to paralyse it; then enzymes dissolve the victim into liquid, which is sucked up by the spider.

A taste of its own medicine: a paralysing sting from a wasp keeps a spider alive while the wasp lay eggs in the victim, which will use the stunned insect for food.

The praying mantis has excellent vision and an extremely fast claw for hooking and grabbing prey.

At the Moruga Bouffe 'mud volcano', saline water mixed with light methanol gas is pushed up from thousands of feet below the surface.

The quenk, a small wild
pig, is hunted for its
meat.

The buffalypso, seen here
on a farm in Tablelands, was
bred in Trinidad.

Fertile farm lands in
Manzanilla, on the east
coast of Trinidad.

Trinidad produces some of the world's best cocoa,
though the 'glory days' of the industry are long gone:
cocoa before being turned to powder.

Raw sugar cane,
freshly cut near
Chaguanas.

Clockwise from top left Sugar cane fields in bloom on Trinidad's central Caroni Plains ... burning off weeds from the fields before cutting ... a master rum barrel maker at the House of Angostura ... cane cutters start work as early as 4 a.m., to beat the hot sun.

Savouring the fresh thyme grown on the Paramin Hills.

Sunrise at Paramin, the hill village north of Port of Spain.

Above Dawn breaks over the palm-lined coast at Mayaro.

Overleaf A severe dry season can trigger serious fires, like this one on the hillsides at Glencoe.

WATER

Tide Running,
Oonya Kempadoo
(2001)

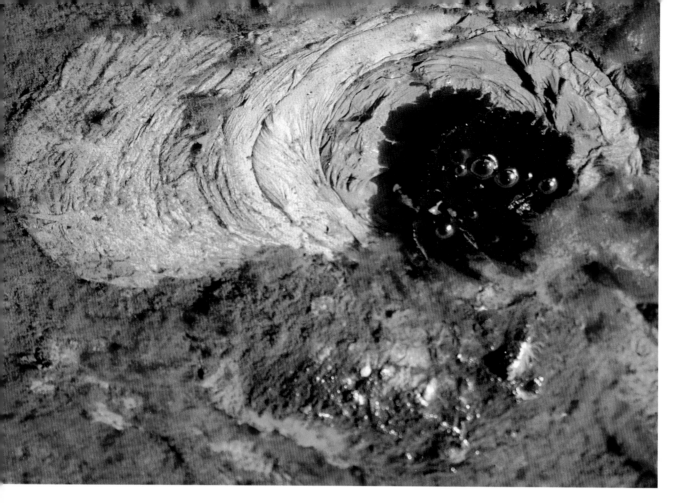

Previous The Pitch Lake at La Brea, its surface partly covered with water: the 'pitch' is a flow of slowly swirling bitumen leaking from a subterranean fault, and is exported to be used on road and roof surfaces in many countries.

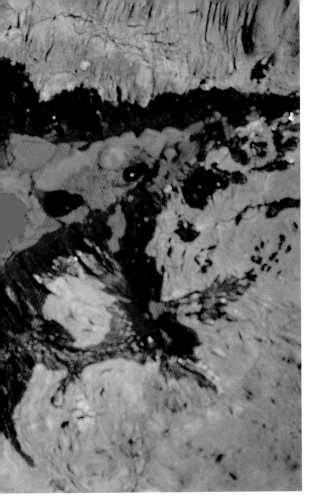

Above Pitch congeals into the strangest formations as it floats to the top and makes contact with water.

Left Just below the surface, sharp fissures can be seen in the tar, and tiny fish and insects flourish in the chemical-heavy water.

Right Jumping Wabine.

Beetle larvae.

These water bugs prey on smaller fish.

Stephen Broadbridge

Above Scarlet ibis fly home to roost at dusk in the Nariva Swamp.

Below A caiman keeps a cautious eye out for prey.

Right Mangrove trees in the Oropuche Lagoon.

Stephen Broadbridge

A first dip at
Blanchisseuse.

Ana takes a swing in a
north coast river.

Left In Tobago, you are never far from the sea, and an offshore cruise is part of many visitors' itineraries.

Right At Pigeon Point, thatched huts invite families to settle down and relax for the day.

Overleaf Sunset at Maracas Bay, the nearest large beach to Port of Spain.

A bottlenose dolphin cruises off Gasparee Island.

Sperm whales off
Trinidad's east coast.

A manta ray at
Speyside, Tobago.

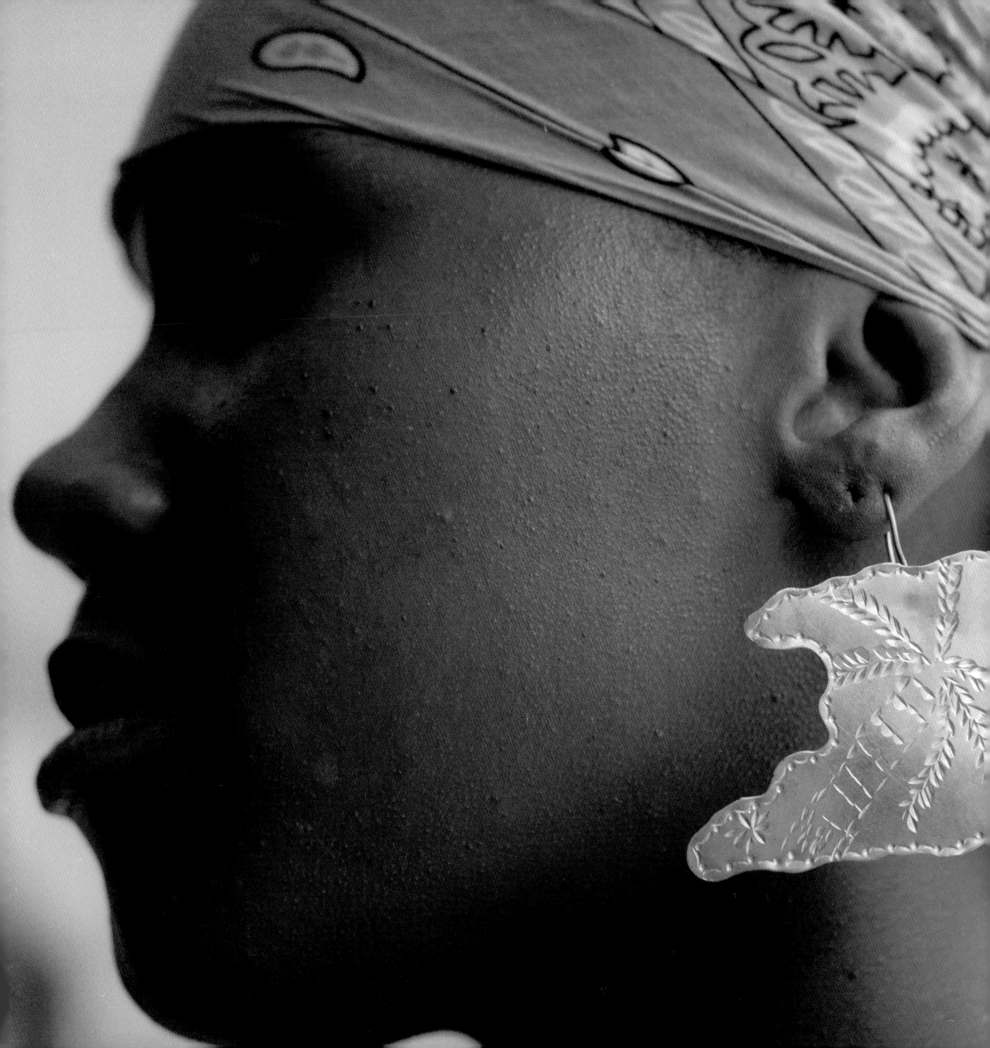

PEOPLE

Merle Hodge, "The
Peoples of Trinidad
& Tobago", in *David
Frost Introduces
Trinidad and Tobago*,
ed. Anthony and
Carr (1975)

Perhaps the epitome of a Trinidadian is the child in the third row of the class with a dark skin and crinkly plaits who looks at you out of decidedly Chinese eyes and announces her name as Jacqueline Maharaj. The strains which converge in her may be African, Indian, Chinese, French, Spanish. She speaks English — will speak standard English on occasion—but is most comfortable in a dialect of English which bears the imprint of French, Spanish, Hindi and West African influences and is the common property of all her variegated classmates.

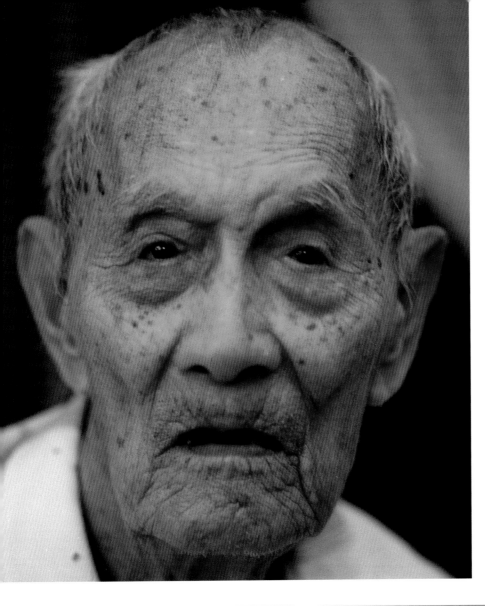

A quiet Sunday morning
in Charlotteville, at
the northern end of
Tobago; a young child
peers out to see if
anything's happening.

Isabelle enjoys home-
made ice cream
between rehearsals.

Thora Dumbell (Auntie Thora), once a prominent dancer herself, has been teaching children ballet for decades.

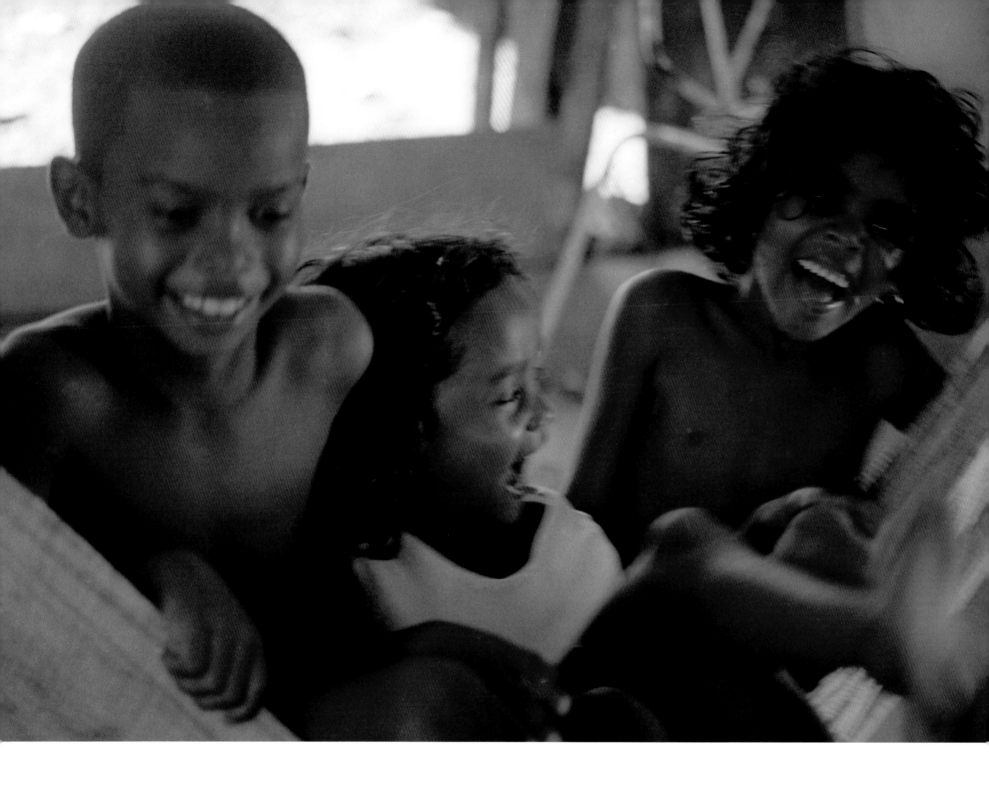

Children enjoy a swing
at Fishermen's Village,
Maracas.

Grave diggers scrub down at the end of a shift at the Lapeyrouse Cemetery in Port of Spain.

Distinctive pleasures:
worn in Morvant **(left)**,
inhaled in Laventille **(right)**.

Left Preparing to face the day in Tobago.

Right Hair and nail parlours are important in a woman's life here on George Street in Port of Spain.

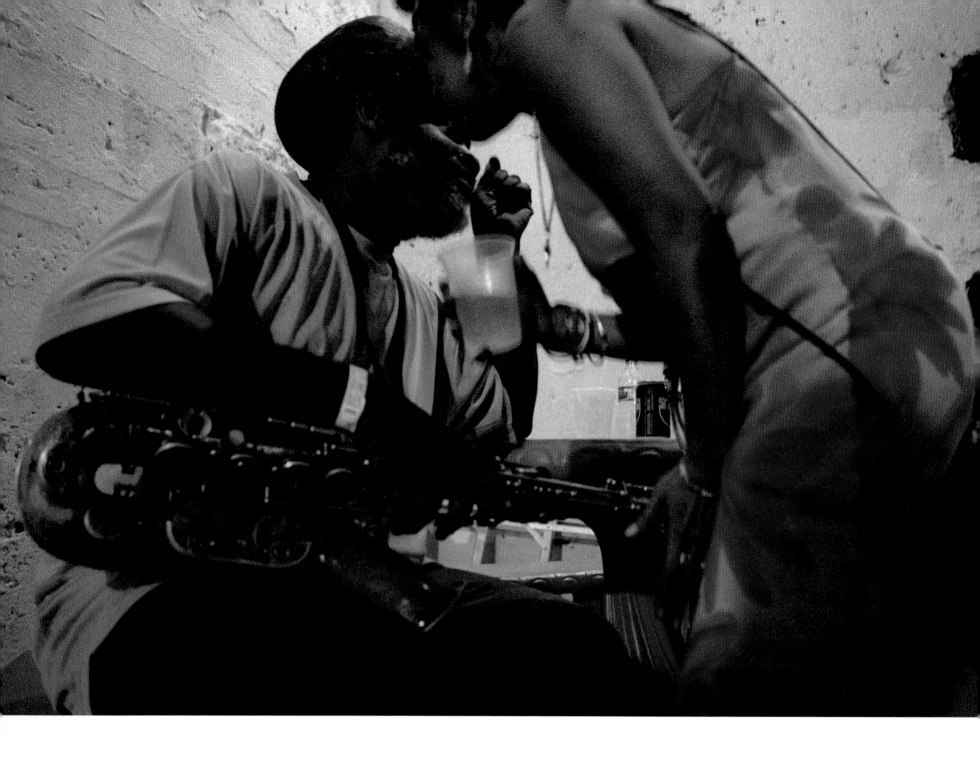

Musicians confer
backstage at a reggae
concert staged in a
downtown car park.

At the Kavmar ballroom dancing club on Henry Street, Port of Spain, a gentleman must know the proper way to ask a lady to dance.

At Buccoo in Tobago, goat racing is a well established Easter tradition, reputedly as a retort to the fancy horse-racing crowd in Trinidad.

Warming up at Santa Rosa. This international track replaced local tracks in Tobago, south Trinidad and Port of Spain (where racing used to take place on the Queen's Park Savannah).

A car sound-off
competition at Waller
Field.

A clean-up by the
Valencia River.

A family outing to Port
of Spain pauses at the
lookout on Lady Young
Road, which offers one
of the best views of
the city.

A cold beer at the
beach, Chaguaramas.

The lure of speed. Drag
racing at Waller Field.

The Great Race for power boats is held at the end of August, following a choppy course from the Yacht Club near Port of Spain to Store Bay in Tobago.

Sporting heroes:
Sprinter Ato Boldon has
won silver and bronze
in the 100m and 200m
sprints at the Olympics.

Trinidadian cricketer Brian Lara has twice broken the record for the highest score ever made in Test cricket: here he kisses the ground in Antigua after making 400 not out in 2004.

George Bovell III took a bronze medal in the 200m individual medley at the 2004 Olympics in Athens.

Designer Peter Minshall began to re-energise Carnival costume design in 1976 with "Paradise Lost", and brought Carnival-based design to the Barcelona and Atlanta Olympics.

Shirley Bahadur

Ulric Cross
– former judge, high
commissioner, RAF
officer and much else
– enjoys a game of
tennis at the Country
Club.

Ingenious local handicraft can be found on several beaches in Tobago, like The Naturalist's at Pigeon Point.

Watching the sunset at Store Bay, Tobago.

Eamon makes and sells
hand-crafted jewellery
in Tobago.

This US visitor returns
every year to fish at
Crown Point, Tobago.

Talparo: a place in the country.

His sight is gone, but this Blanchisseuse man's keen hearing will ensure that he greets you in the old village.

The offshore island of
Chacachacare once
hosted a leprosarium.
Long abandoned,
its chapel and other
buildings are still there.

The apartment of art
dealer Mark Pereira
enjoys spectacular
views over the capital,
Port of Spain.

Entering the capital
on the fast-moving
Beetham Highway.

Methanol, ammonia, urea, steel – the massive Point Lisas industrial estate on Trinidad's west coast, fuelled by offshore natural gas, is the country's industrial heart. Further down the coast, natural gas liquefaction and aluminium smelting are being added to the mix.

A large cruise liner docked at Port of Spain's cruise ship complex.

A violinist serenades passers-by on
their way home after work.

Shopping in downtown
Port of Spain.

Cell blocks and store rooms can still be seen at Fort George, 1,100 feet above Port of Spain. A major defensive battery, it never saw action, and today provides spectacular views over the city and the surrounding coastline.

The Globe cinema
at Green Corner
symbolises the old,
familiar Port of Spain.

Along the western side of the Queen's Park Savannah, seven century-old colonial mansions ('the Magnificent Seven') display all the lavishness and extravagance of turn-of-the century colonial architecture.

Whitehall, the office of the Prime Minister.

The Queen's Park Savannah at sunrise.

Stollmeyer's Castle, or Killarney, now an adjunct of the Prime Minister's Whitehall office next door.

Queen's Royal College (1904): this is where Trinidad and Tobago's first prime minister (Dr Eric Williams) and its most famous writer (V. S. Naipaul) both went to school.

Left Hot pepper sauce comes in many forms.

Right Good Chinese restaurants abound. Soong's, in San Fernando, was one of the first and is still considered one of the best. A new generation of Chinese chefs has been making its mark in Trinidad, bringing excellent new cuisine.

The cemetery at
St Joseph (the first
capital of Trinidad)
is lit by hundreds of
candles on All Saints'
Day.

Sacred fire at the
Edinburgh village
Hindu temple

An elder of the Orisha faith (above) at a gathering in Debe (right). Orisha, an African
belief system that has incorporated certain Christian figures, is widespread but
low-profile; it is close to similar traditions in Brazil, Haiti and Cuba.

Below **A Hindu cremation on the shore at Waterloo, on Trinidad's east coast. Beyond** is a renovated temple originally built in the sea by a devout sugar worker who was denied permission to build on land.

Right **'Spinning the moon'** at the Hosay festival in St James, a western suburb of Port of Spain. Hosay, a Shi'ite festival marking the death of the Prophet's grandson at the Battle of Kerbala in 682, is frowned on by Sunni Muslims, but has been embraced by Trinidadians. Dancers spin two heavy 'moons' like this one on their shoulders, representing the martyred Hussein and his brother.

Participants in
the Ganga Dharaa
River festival at
Blanchisseuse, a
local version of
rituals performed in
India in the Ganges;
in Trinidad the
Marianne River is
used.

Above Hindu worshippers reach a trance-like state as they dance in the sea at Carenage.

Below Bobo Shanti Rastafarians hold in an all-night vigil in their St Joseph tabernacle in honour of the birthday of the late emperor Haile Selassie I of Ethiopia.

Right The Ganga Dharaa festival at Blanchisseuse.

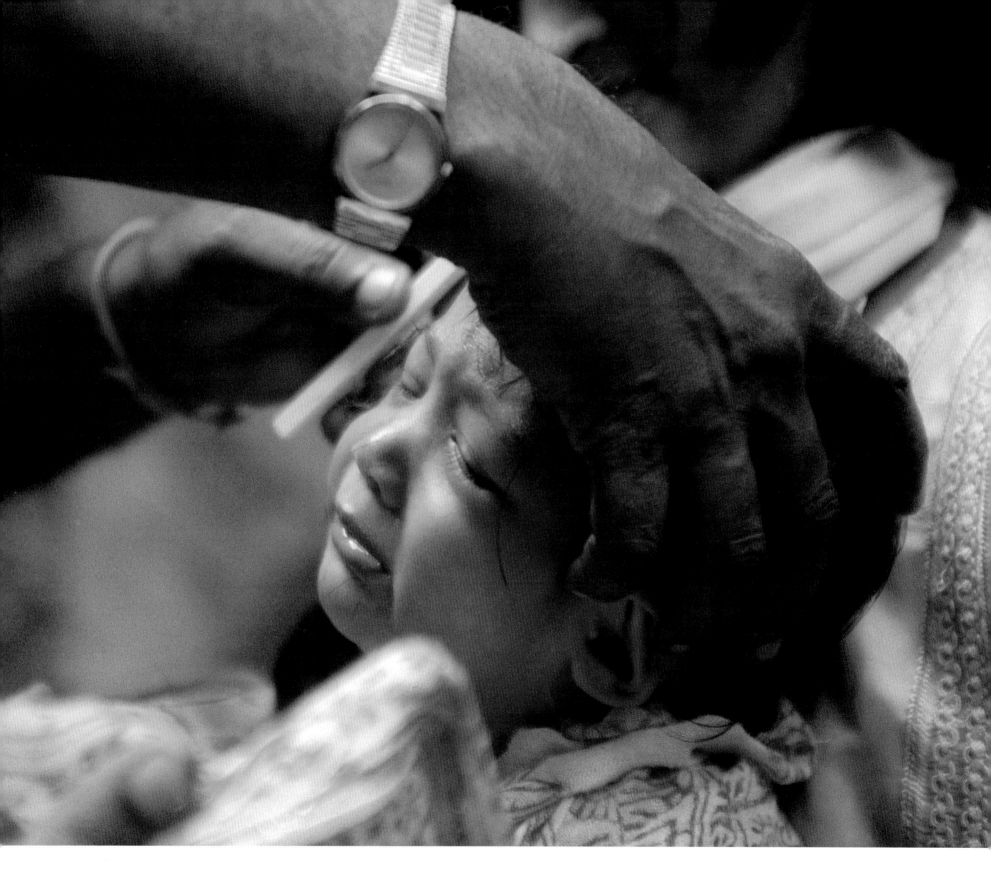

An Indian wedding in Trinidad is a lavish and protracted affair;
here a bride prepares for her wedding in Cunupia.

Benedictine monks first established themselves in Trinidad in 1912, and built a monastery 800 feet up in the foothills of the Northern Range, with magnificent views over the central part of the island. Mount St Benedict includes a seminary, a vocational school and an attractive guest house; the monks produce home-made yogurt.

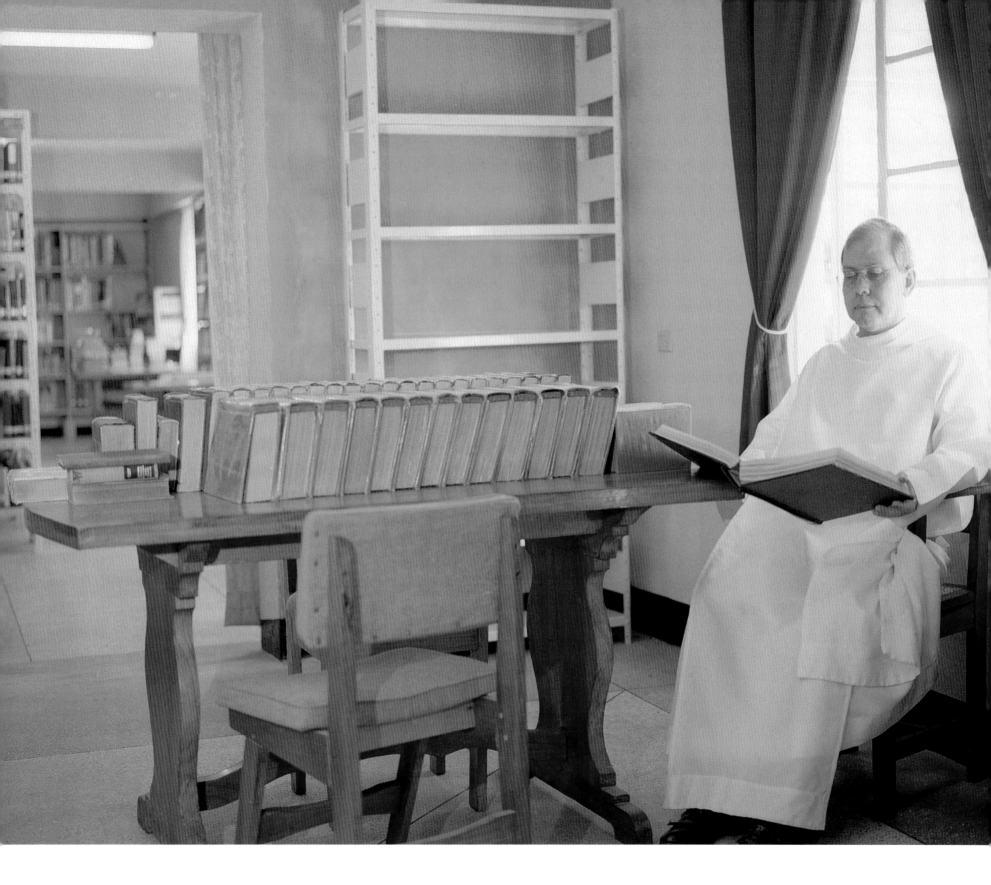

Barbara Burke **(opposite page)** is archbishop of Trinidad's Spiritual or
Shouter Baptists **(above)**, a substantial indigenous church similar to
the Revival movement in Jamaica and the Shakers in St Vincent.

Young Muslim girls
sleep in the afternoon
silence of a mosque.

AFTERWORD

Light was my constant nemesis. It is the element I lived for, studied and looked at from every angle and intensity. Light is why I woke up at 4 a.m. and it was what I was chasing around for in the long shadows at dusk. I soon grew a love-hate relationship with Trinidad's weather. Six months of rain, which produces dark, grey, cloudy light, or six months of sun, which produces bright, dusty, hazy light – both a photographer's nightmare. But after a while, I became more in-tune with the environment. I knew during wet season I had to be up at sunrise, and got deep, clear blue sky; in dry season, after 4 p.m. a stunning orange glow would creep in from the west. It is at these times that I would go to work, either skulking around Port of Spain with a small camera and one lens or lugging a tripod and many lenses up a hill for a view.

This book has neither political nor racial nor religious affiliations. The political T-shirts and badges are remnants of three elections in two years, which people are now content to let filter into normal everyday garments. I apologise that not every function, worship, ceremony, tone and hue could be presented equally. At the editing stage we tried to be balanced and concentrate on the quality and excitement that each image holds, rather than the constant need for political correctness.

What this book is trying to be is an honest look at where we are today, how we got here and what the future holds for us. Our twin-island nation is in a massive sea of change, which we see everyday in Port of Spain or on the Tobago coastlines. Yet in the villages of the northeast or of southern Trinidad, people are living a slight variation of the lives of their forefathers; the fashions change but the lifestyle remains.

I love Trinidad and Tobago.

I have been coming to Trinidad since I was a child. I learned to walk on its hot tarmac; as a toddler with oversized trunks, I was tossed by Maracas surf. At fifteen, I stole a first kiss. At eighteen, with my first camera, I was hustling away downtown shooting black and white film of vendors. I always dreamed of doing a book here. Starting at the turn of the millennium, this is the result of four years of photographing and production.

I used Kodak Portra 160 and 400 ASA film, 35 and 120 format. Both of these keep excellent grain and quality and vivid colours, and are versatile in exposure control in difficult lighting situations. Sometimes, shoots were planned in advance; many times I would choose an area and wander around just shooting and meeting people. Some shoots took a year to organise, but many were pure serendipity – when all elements of light, action and my position collided into one.

My worst experience was probably discovering that burrowing-biting water bugs inhabit the Pitch Lake. I had to pull them off me after each time I immersed myself. But apart from broken car exhaust silencers from potholes, numerous flat tyres – including one being bitten by a dog – three smashed lenses, one dropped camera body and a dose of bet-rouge, I stayed incident-free.

A fun episode was losing my favourite sandal after a Tobago dog walked off with it. It caused hysterics as I walked down the high street with one bare foot, asking people for a shoe shop and having to explain the story each time. It was actually returned to me several months later, when a friend retrieved it and brought it all the way to town on his next visit, although it was a little frayed at the edges.

There were so many fantastic high points and experiences, but one of the most endearing happened on near completion of the book. While covering the declining numbers of cocoa workers in Couva, a meal of chicken and rice and extremely hot pepper was handed to me. We talked of farming, country life and English football. One of the women giggled and whispered to her husband, 'Look, he eat like one of us'. I'm still not sure how they expected me to eat but I must have been hiding the flames in my mouth pretty well. It seemed to summarise the end of my journey very well. I had found the Trinidad I was looking for and, more importantly, the Trinidad that people need to remember.

Acknowledgements

This project was just a dream a few years ago. The people below made this dream a reality. I wish to thank:

Candyce Kelshall for being my first point of contact – her energy and enthusiasm persuaded me to follow through; her former Director, Dr Carla Noel, for arranging logistics to get me here to start in 2000; Tony Poyer for providing my first tours; Tricia Lee Kelshall and her parents for their unlimited generous hospitality; Mark Lyndersay and Donna, who not only provided a studio and office space – which soon became a second home – but also equipped me with professional advice, on-hand Mac computer expertise, and even the odd plate of food; Jason and Bobby at Script J, whose early interest and printing of promotional material were fundamental in this project from the start; Digital Graphics – Ernie, Shiyam and team – for early friendship and support.

Steven Delacosta of Film Processors, whose staff shuddered each time I came in with a bulging bag of film. My demands on quality, speed and service were consistently met throughout the duration. The *Guardian* newspaper, whose former editor, Lennox Grant, provided local Press accreditation, and Marlon Rouse, director of photography, for like-minded talks; the team at the photo desk – thanks for making me feel one of the family; music photographer David Wears, whose openness, logistical help and pre-social event warnings made the Carnival section of this book possible; Tony, Brendan & Damian Baylis of TATEC for logistical help for 'The Magnificent Seven' building images; Nicole Freakly; Go Graphics; Sacha; MEP team; Brown Associates; Simone at Insights; Angela Fox for press assistance at Carnival for the last few years.

Barbara Jenkins and Dylan Kerrigan for their research and vast contact base, which was waiting for me when I first arrived; Piero at Mt Plaisir for his professional advice and criticism after looking at hundreds of pre-edited images, in wonderful surroundings accompanied by delicious food; Abigail Hadeed also for her sharp eye at editing; Ataklan, dread – your personal friendship gave grounding, your music gave me strength – whose persona ensured safe passage working in Laventille and Morvant; Pigeon, for his equal guidance and introduction to the stunning, understated area of Belmont; Bianca in Sea Lots, whose smile opened doors and whose food hit the spot; Amy, for showing me Maloney.

Roger at Enchanted Waters Hotel, Tobago, for help with accommodation; Ron Tiah, who introduced me to scuba diving and the underwater world many years ago and was actually a catalyst to my current career; the Crooks family, who allowed me to be present at a difficult personal family loss; Clark at Tobago Sea Kayak in Charlotteville for the expeditions; Dougies Guest House in Manzanilla; Pat Turpin & Caroline for Charlotteville; Mr Sonny and his goats – Red Rum, Uday and Mokatika – at Buccoo village.

Gaylord at the Military Museum for historical background; Edward Hernandez at Tobago Museum; Raj Pooran, the collector at the University of the West Indies, for access and handling of the Natural Science Archive; Sheeba, who introduced me to tree climbing and the rainforest canopy; Jal Khan and Edmond, my first guides, who were always willing to wake at the crack of dawn and get wet in a jungle somewhere; Dr Victor Quesnel who had many of the bugs and insects living in his own bush garden, which he studies tirelessly; Ira Mathur who reviewed the growth of this project at many stages – her advice and compliments were essential.

Skye Hernandez & Georgia Popplewell of Tangerine for the daunting task and late nights of editing thousands of images; designer Gareth Jenkins for his exciting and creative layouts and bringing the book to life.

All the personal friends whose help, advice and encouragement got me through: Tracey Malleilou, Jason Kelshall, Justin, Wyatt Gallery, Steve Voss, Sean Drakes, Raff & Laurent; my own family network of Quesnels and Baylis's, whom I always knew I could call on in an emergency or just for a fresh juice; Charlotte Galt, King George, Eamon, Chi, Neysha and her bevy of girls; Jill Waddell and Dominique for their encouragement at the last stage; Jethro Sheeran for company, friendship and assisting on my first trip.

Nick Gillard from Macmillan whose vision and trust in me gave me this opportunity.

To my family, I can never thank you enough, for implanting the good memories of childhood trips to Trinidad and for all the years of support even with my constant absence on foreign assignments.

Most of all, thanks to the hundreds of beautiful people of Trinidad and Tobago who let me work freely among them. I gate-crashed their *limes* (meetings), slept on their beds, danced, drank, and ate their food. I can only hope I have done justice representing your islands through my camera.

Alex Smailes
Port of Spain 2006

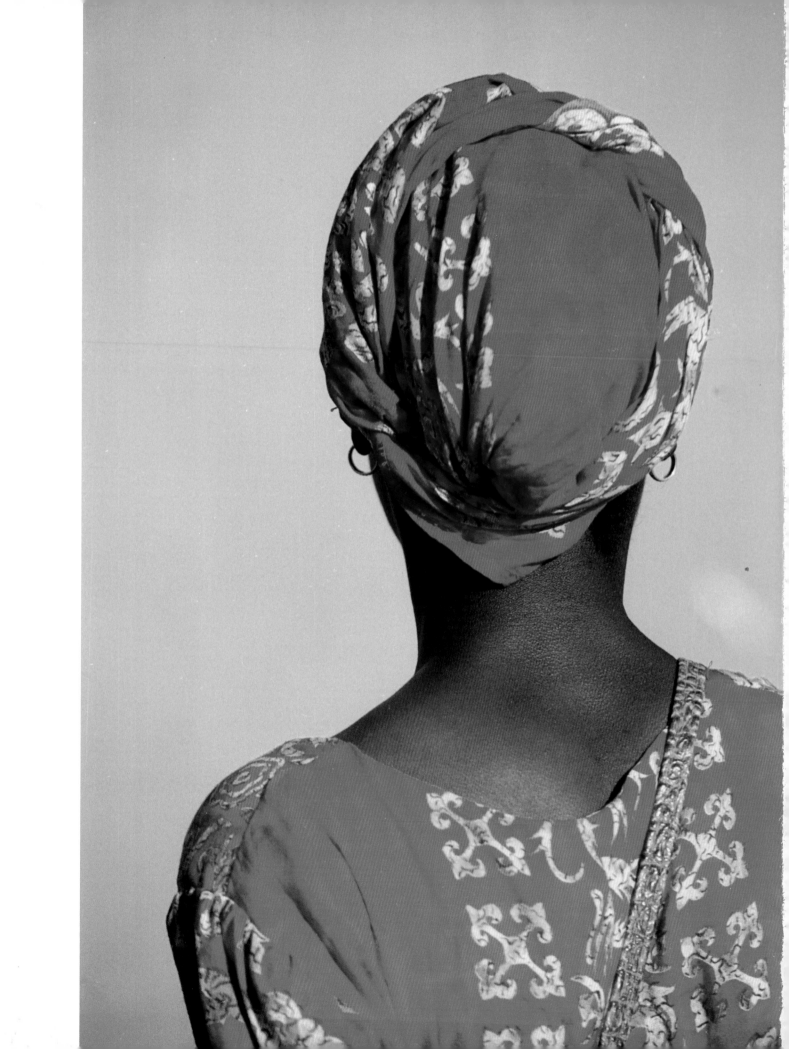